A Crabtree Roots Book
Un libro de Las Raíces de Crab

FARM ANIMAL FRIENDS
Animales de granja amistosos

PIGS
CERDOS

AMY CULLIFORD
SANTIAGO OCHOA

Crabtree Publishing
crabtreebooks.com

School-to-Home Support for Caregivers and Teachers

This book helps children grow by letting them practice reading. Here are a few guiding questions to help the reader with building his or her comprehension skills. Possible answers appear here in red.

Before Reading:

- What do I think this book is about?
  - *This book is about pigs.*
  - *This book is about pigs that live on farms.*

- What do I want to learn about this topic?
  - *I want to learn what pigs eat.*
  - *I want to learn what colors a pig can be.*

During Reading:

- I wonder why...
  - *I wonder why some pigs are pink.*
  - *I wonder why pigs say oink.*

- What have I learned so far?
  - *I have learned that pigs can be big or little.*
  - *I have learned that pigs can be different colors.*

After Reading:

- What details did I learn about this topic?
  - *I have learned that pigs can have spots.*
  - *I have learned that pigs eat a lot.*

- Read the book again and look for the vocabulary words.
  - *I see the word **pink** on page 8 and the word **spots** on page 10. The other vocabulary words are found on page 14.*

This is a **pig**.

Este es un **cerdo**.

Some pigs are big.

Algunos cerdos son grandes.

Some pigs are little.

Algunos cerdos son pequeños.

Pigs can be **pink**, black, or brown.

Los cerdos pueden ser **rosados**, negros o cafés.

Some pigs have **spots**!

¡Algunos cerdos tienen **manchas**!

Pigs eat all day long.

Los cerdos comen todo el día.

All pigs say, *oink*!

Todos los cerdos dicen *¡oink!*

Words to Know
Palabras para aprender

pig
cerdo

pink
manchas

spots
rosados

32 Words

This is a **pig**.

Some pigs are big.

Some pigs are little.

Pigs can be **pink**, black, or brown.

Some pigs have **spots**!

Pigs eat all day long.

All pigs say, *oink*!

35 palabras

Este es un **cerdo**.

Algunos cerdos son grandes.

Algunos cerdos son pequeños.

Los cerdos pueden ser **rosados**, negros o cafés.

¡Algunos cerdos tienen **manchas**!

Los cerdos comen todo el día.

Todos los cerdos dicen *¡oink!*

FARM ANIMAL FRIENDS
Animales de granja amistosos

PIGS
CERDOS

Crabtree Publishing

crabtreebooks.com 800-387-7650

Written by: Amy Culliford
Translation by: Santiago Ochoa
Designed by: Rhea Wallace
Series Development: James Earley
Proofreader: Kathy Middleton
Educational Consultant: Christina Lemke M.Ed.
Production manager: Candice Campbell
Photographs: Shutterstock: Irina Kozorog: cover (tl); Alexander Raths: cover (tr); ArtbyPixel: cover (b); ccpixxphotography: p. 1; Konmac: p. 3, 4-5, 14; sinagra ie: p. 7; C.Lotongkum: p. 9 (t), 14; Juan Aunion: p. 9 (b); acceptphoto: p. 10-11, 14; QiuJu Song: p. 12; Eric Buermeyer: p. 13

Published in Canada
Crabtree Publishing
616 Welland Ave.
St. Catharines, Ontario
L2M 5V6

Published in the United States
Crabtree Publishing
347 Fifth Avenue,
Suite 1402-145
New York, NY, 10016

Library and Archives Canada Cataloguing in Publication
Available at the Library and Archives Canada

Library of Congress Cataloging-in-Publication Data
Available at the Library of Congress

Paperback: 9781039624474
Ebook: 9781039625310
Epub: 9781039624894

Printed in the U.S.A./092025/CP20250918